MADONNA

SMITHMARK

MADONNA

'I know the aspect of my personality, being the vixen, the heart-breaker and the incredibly provocative girl is a very marketable image. But it's not insincere. You just can't take it seriously.'

Marie Cahill

SMITHMARK

Published by Smithmark Publishers
112 Madison Avenue
New York, New York 10016

Produced by
Brompton Books Corp.
15 Sherwood Place
Greenwich, CT 06830

ISBN 0-8317-5705-1

Printed in Hong Kong

10 9 8 7 6 5 4 3 2

Reprinted 1991

Designed by Ruth DeJauregui

Page 1: Madonna is a woman of many faces, many images. In her *True Blue* era, she adopted an innocent yet sensuous demeanor.

Page 3: In *Who's That Girl?* Madonna played the part of the wacky blond.

These pages: A look at the early Madonna.

Contents

Introduction

She is the world's most exciting star, known across the world by just a single word—Madonna, a name which conjures up a mysterious amalgam of the reverent and the irreverent.

Sexy and sultry, she exploded onto the pop music scene in 1983 with her debut album, *Madonna*. Soon to follow was a succession of hit singles and albums. From *Like a Virgin* (1984) to *I'm Breathless* (1990), every Madonna album hit the top of the charts. She has had 18 consecutive top five hits, with worldwide sales of 60 million.

Driven by a disco beat, her music is bright and sparkling, but what really made Madonna a star was her provocative and mercurial image. Her music videos portray her as the material girl, the blond bombshell, or the not-so-virginal virgin. Famous for wearing lacy underwear as outerwear, Madonna quickly became the hottest sex symbol since Marilyn Monroe, but unlike the tragic Marilyn, Madonna was nobody's victim. This lady is sexy *and* shrewd.

She has parlayed her talents beyond the music world with a critically acclaimed performance in the movie *Desperately Seeking Susan* (1985), in which she played the part of the bold, self-assured Susan. Though her next two feature films—*Shanghai Surprise* (1986) and *Who's That Girl?* (1987)—were box office flops, Madonna would shine on Broadway in David Mamet's *Speed-the-Plow* (1988),

Right: In 1983, Madonna set the pop world on fire with her music *and* her funky but sexy image.

Left: Two years later, her singing career going strong, she landed the title role in *Desperately Seeking Susan.*

6

Left: Madonna—the glamour girl.

Right: Her hair dyed platinum blond, Madonna was compared to another sexy blond bombshell—Marilyn Monroe.

Below: Madonna as the seductive Breathless Mahoney, with Warren Beatty, in *Dick Tracy*.

her most serious role and one decidedly different from her previous roles.

Once again on the silver screen, she sizzled in the part of Breathless Mahoney, the sexy and villaincus nightclub singer in *Dick Tracy* (1990). Though the part seemed tailor-made for her, Madonna considered the part 'no great stretch' and formed her own production company to find more challenging roles for her. Off screen, Madonna's romance with co-star and director Warren Beatty gave the gossip columnists plenty to talk about.

While *Dick Tracy* was packing the movie theaters in the United States, Madonna was taking the rest of the world by storm with her Blond Ambition Tour. Her third and most exciting tour to date, the seductive and glitzy show was fast-paced and tightly choreographed—more like a Broadway production than a rock concert.

Though all her shows were sellouts, not everyone liked or even approved of the sultry queen of pop. In Italy, her overt sexual behavior created a scandal. Nevertheless, Madonna is a woman who makes no excuses. She met the criticism head on and welcomed her detractors to her show.

Madonna has come a long way since she first started singing in New York discos. Whether she is acting or singing, Madonna will continue to be one of the brightest stars of the 1990s.

The Girl from Bay City, Michigan

Yes, her name really is Madonna. When she was just beginning to establish herself, people assumed that she had chosen the name for its glamourous sound, but the truth is that she was named for her mother.

Madonna Louise Veronica Ciccone was born on 16 August 1958 in Bay City, Michigan. The oldest girl in a family of six, she had to face heartache at an early age. Just before her seventh birthday, her mother died of breast cancer.

Her grief-stricken father felt unable to cope with the demands of a full-time job while caring for the children, so with a heavy heart he sent them to live with relatives. As soon as possible, the family was reunited, but much to the children's surprise, their 'housekeeper' was to become their new mother, and Madonna's father and his new wife would soon have two more children of their own.

Years later Madonna was still trying to cope with her mother's death. 'I had to deal with the loss of my mother, then I had to deal with the guilt of her being gone, and then

Back in 1976, Madonna's friends from Rochester Adams High School never dreamed that their classmate (*left*) would someday be rich and famous, but Madonna's success came as no surprise to her. She worked hard to achieve it!

Above and right: Two of Madonna's funkier looks.

10

Left: Healthy? You bet she is. Madonna attacks fitness with her usual fervor. Her daily workout includes aerobics, swimming and a six-mile run.

Right: Madonna is as smart as she is talented and since the start of her career, she has used the media to her best advantage.

I had to deal with the loss of my father when he married my stepmother. So I was just one angry, abandoned little girl. I'm still angry.' The video for the song 'Oh Father,' in which she is seen dancing on her mother's grave, is described as Madonna's 'attempt to embrace and accept' her mother's death.

As the oldest girl, Madonna was responsible for many household chores, especially caring for her younger siblings. Later in life, Madonna would say, 'I really saw myself as the quintessential Cinderella. You know, I have this stepmother and I have all this work to do and it's awful and I never go out and I don't have any pretty dresses.'

In spite of the heavy load she carried at home, Madonna always earned good grades in school. A conscientious student, Madonna was well-liked by the nuns, but there was one thing Madonna didn't like about school and that was the uniforms. She found them boring and drab, so Madonna sought new ways to add a little flair—bows in her hair or strange-colored knee socks. And thus began Madonna's eclectic and flamboyant style of dressing that has become her hallmark today.

Clothes were just one way to attract attention. Never one to shy away from the spotlight, Madonna signed up for every school play or musical. At home, she and her friends danced to Motown hits in the backyard, but dancing was more than just fun. Dance became the consuming interest of her adolescence. She arranged to finish her classes early in the day so she could study ballet after school. Her ballet teacher and mentor, Christopher Flynn, saw something special in Madonna and encouraged her to go to New York to pursue a career as a dancer.

After Madonna graduated from Rochester Adams High School in 1976, she won a full, four-year dance scholarship to the University of Michigan, but the glamour of New York and its promise of fame beckoned, and, much to her father's dismay, she dropped out of college. Low on cash

These pages: Madonna's fascination with crucifixes dates back to her years in Catholic schools. 'There's something very mysterious and alluring about it,' says Madonna. Church leaders, however, object to Madonna's use of a crucifix as jewelry, and in 1990 tried to ban her concerts in Italy.

but high on determination, Madonna boarded a plane for New York, where she won a scholarship to the highly acclaimed Alvin Ailey School.

Although she was a talented dancer, Madonna was just one of many dancers at Alvin Ailey. Everyone was so serious and intent that she found herself rebelling against the discipline, just as she rebelled against her school uniform a decade before. She dyed her hair bright colors and ripped her leotard and pinned it back together with safety pins. Eventually, Madonna realized she didn't have the patience to wait years to make it big and decided to look for other ways to express her creative energies—and so she turned to music.

At a party, Madonna met Dan Gilroy, a musician based in Queens. A romance blossomed and Madonna eventually moved in with him. His apartment, which doubled as his studio, was an abandoned synagogue, where Dan taught her how to play the guitar. Driven by her desire to succeed, she started writing songs and learning how to play other musical instruments. After this year-long period, a time Madonna refers to as her 'intensive musical training,' the Breakfast Club was born. The fledgling band consisted of Dan and his brother Ed, with Madonna on drums and fellow ex-dancer Angie Smit on bass.

Though the Gilroys had been in the music business for years, they lacked something that Madonna had in abundance: moxie. As Gilroy recalls: 'She'd be up in the morning, a quick cup of coffee, then right to the phones, calling up everybody—everybody. Everyone from [local record dealer] Bleeker Bob's to potential management.'

From the beginning, Madonna was aiming for the top. She wanted record deals—and she wanted to sing. It was time for Madonna and the Breakfast Club to go their separate ways.

Madonna soon returned to Manhattan and promptly formed her own band. She soon came to the attention of Mark Kamins, a deejay at Danceteria—which was then known as *the* place to be. 'She had her own style,' Kamins recalled. 'When she'd start dancing, there'd be 20 people up and dancing with her.'

After hearing one of Madonna's demo tapes, Kamins was so impressed that he played it at Danceteria. More importantly, Kamins took Madonna to the studio and produced an improved version of the demo, which he then presented to Sire Records and arranged a record deal for her. The song—'Everybody,' a funky dance tune—went nowhere on the charts but it launched Madonna's recording career.

15

These pages: Madonna—about the time her first album was released. Little did the world know that Madonna would soon become the most exciting star on the planet.

Soon after her first album hit the top of the charts, Madonna was making fashion news as well as music news. Her daring style of clothing inspired thousands of teenagers across the United States to dress just like her.

Madonna— the first album

In July 1983, Sire released Madonna's first album, entitled *Madonna*. 'Holiday,' the LP's first single, was released the following December and stayed on the charts for 11 weeks, peaking at #16. 'Holiday,' a sparkling tune, was produced by the man who had replaced Gilroy as Madonna's current flame, John 'Jellybean' Benitez.

Benitez, a hotshot deejay at the Funhouse, had made a name for himself remixing demo tapes of up and coming stars. Jellybean captured Madonna's heart, as well as her sound, and the couple stayed together for two years.

Although her debut album got off to a slow start in 1983, Madonna, as always, was confident. 'I know this record is good, and one of these days Warner Bros [Sire's parent company] and the rest of them are going to figure it out.'

It didn't take long for the world to discover *Madonna* and Madonna. Two more singles from *Madonna* were released in 1984. 'Borderline' made it to the top ten, and 'Lucky Star,' her biggest hit thus far, peaked at #4. By the fall of 1984, *Madonna* had gone gold and eventually would go platinum. The album sold three million copies, and her next one would sell twice as many.

Left: The jacket of Madonna's debut album—*Madonna*. The album yielded 'Borderline,' the first of Madonna's top ten singles.

Right: At first, the critics dismissed Madonna as a disco diva whose success would be short-lived.

Above: Madonna's first love is dance and all her concert tours have featured exciting and, in some cases, erotic dance numbers.

Left: The photo of Madonna on the back cover of *Madonna* is as equally alluring as the photo on the front.

Right: The sultry singer.

20

Like A Virgin

A savvy businesswoman, Madonna surrounded herself with the best people in the industry. She hired Freddy DeMann, Michael Jackson's manager, to manage her career. At that time, Michael Jackson was the biggest star around. Then, she hired Nile Rodgers, the producer of David Bowie's wildly successful *Let's Dance*, to produce her second album, *Like A Virgin*.

The first single released from *Like A Virgin* was the title song. Released on 17 November 1984, it reached #1 by December 22. The new year began with everyone listening to 'Like A Virgin.' 'Material Girl' peaked at #2 and the album itself hit #1.

Madonna mania had taken the country by storm. As MTV became an integral part of the music business in the mid-1980s, Madonna videos followed on the heels of her hit songs, and Madonna wiggled her way into living rooms across the nation projecting an image of raw sex appeal. In 'Lucky Star' she was unabashedly erotic as she thrust her breasts and bottom at the camera, while in 'Burning Up' she acted as if she was itching to remove her dress.

The self-proclaimed Boy Toy, Madonna's sexpot image may have enraged feminists, but teenagers across the nation adored her and emulated her style of dress. Lace bodices, lacy gloves, micro miniskirts and spiked heels became *de rigueur* for a multitude of Madonna Wanna-Bes. Eletra Casadei, a Los Angeles designer of Madonna-esque clothing, sold $25 million in strapless, lacy dresses under the TD4 ('to die for') label in 1984–the year Madonna first came into the public eye. Fads come and go, and many designers expected the Madonna trend to be short-lived. Much to their amazement, Madonna wear was selling even stronger a year later.

From the beginning of her career, Madonna knew that her image was as important as her musical talents. In true chameleon style, Madonna has never hesitated to alter her image as she sees fit. For the video accompanying

Left: The cover of *Like A Virgin*, the album that propelled Madonna to stardom.

Right: Though she is dressed in white and lace, Madonna is anything but virginal.

22

Left: Attired in her version of a wedding dress, Madonna concluded every concert on her Virgin tour with a steamy encore of 'Like A Virgin.'

The tape of her concert, *The Virgin Tour—Madonna Live,* was the best-selling music videocassette in 1986.

Below: The back cover of *Like A Virgin.*

Right: Madonna in 1985, after *Like A Virgin* had skyrocketed her to fame.

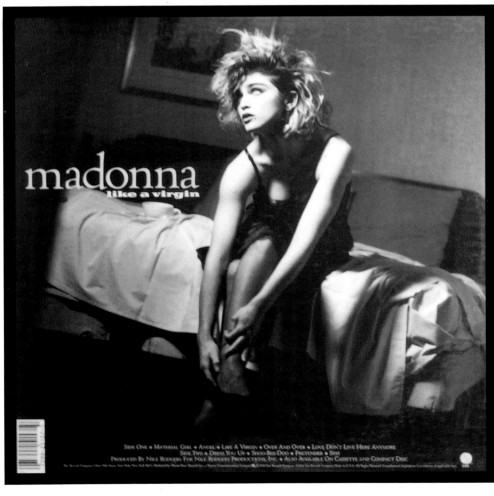

Above: The Material Girl and her inspiration—Marilyn Monroe *(above right)* cooing 'Diamonds Are A Girl's Best Friend' in *Gentlemen Prefer Blondes*.

'Material Girl,' her second single from *Like A Virgin*, Madonna styled herself after Marilyn Monroe's unforgettable performance of 'Diamonds are a Girl's Best Friend' from *Gentlemen Prefer Blondes*. The video naturally invited comparisons between the two glamourous stars, and at first Madonna enjoyed the comparisons: 'I saw it all as a compliment. She was very sexy—extremely sexy—and she had blonde hair, and so on and so forth. Then it started to annoy me, because nobody wants to be continuously compared to someone else. You want people to see that you have a statement of your own to make.'

The difference between the two, as Madonna hastened to point out, is that 'Marilyn Monroe was a victim and I'm not.' Similar sentiments would be echoed later by psychologist Dr Joyce Brothers: 'Madonna is a sexy person for our time. She's independent and on her own two feet. Women like her because they don't feel she's a victim. Men like her because she's sexy, but not straight out, like in *Penthouse*. She is childlike and innocent but at the same time naughty.'

At top: Madonna in a pose reminiscent of Hollywood's Golden Age of Glamour Girls.

Left: After her singles raced to the top of the charts, Madonna soon received praise from her peers at the American Music Awards.

27

Above: Madonna and Huey Lewis at the American Music Awards.

Right: Madonna had plenty to smile about. Her hard work and effort had paid off—she was on her way!

Desperately Seeking Susan

ritics expected Madonna's lucky star to fizzle, like so many pop phenomena's. Madonna, however, proved that she was much more than just a dance club diva. While her second album was climbing the charts, Madonna turned her attention to the silver screen in *Desperately Seeking Susan* (1985). When director Susan Seidelman heard that the hottest singer in town was interested in the part of Susan, she invited Madonna to come in for a screen test. 'She was nervous and vulnerable and not at all arrogant—sweet, but intelligent, with a sense of humor,' recalls Seidelman. 'I just started seeing her as Susan.' The heads at Orion Pictures were reluctant to cast an untested actress, but producer Midge Sanford was captivated: 'She had this presence you couldn't get rid of.'

Desperately Seeking Susan was a low-budget comedy reminiscent of the comedies of the 1930s—but with a heavy dose of satire. The plot revolves around a case of mistaken identity. Roberta, a bored suburban housewife played by

Left: With two successful albums behind her, Madonna was eager to turn to film. In her first movie, she played a part ideally suited to her own personality— Susan in *Desperately Seeking Susan.*

Susan was the sort of character who made herself at home wherever she was, whether it was an old friend's apartment or a new acquaintance's swimming pool (*right*).

Rosanna Arquette, follows the personal ads for news of Susan, a free-spirited young woman with a knack for getting into trouble. After a bump on the head knocks Roberta unconscious, she can't remember who she is, but everyone around her has mistaken her for Susan, so Roberta assumes that she *is* Susan.

The character of Susan has been compared to Madonna herself. Like Madonna, Susan is bold and very self-assured. Anna Levine, who plays Susan's friend Crystal, recalls that Madonna 'had a very clear vision of her character, which other people didn't always have, so they left her as Madonna.' Madonna had considerable control

The plot revolves around the personal ads (*far left*), a pair of ancient Egyptian earrings (*at top*) and Susan's knack for wreaking havoc in the lives of whomever she meets (*left*).

Left: Madonna as Susan and her co-star Rosanna Arquette, who played the part of Roberta, the bored housewife who thinks *she* is Susan after a bump on the head gives her amnesia.

Right: Though there may be similarities between Madonna and the character of Susan, Madonna would be the first person to point out that she is only playing a part—and Susan is *not* Madonna.

over the role: She did her own hair and makeup, and injected Susan with her own brand of self-confidence. Allowing Madonna to express the role in her own way turned out to be a very wise move. *Desperately Seeking Susan* was rush released for the Easter season in 1985 and earned an unexpected $16 million.

Desperately Seeking Susan featured one Madonna song—'Into the Groove,' one of the year's best dance tunes. Just as the movie was released, another Madonna film tune was hitting the top of the charts. 'Crazy for You,' a ballad from the movie *Vision Quest* (1985), hit the #1 spot on 11 May 1985. Though she appeared on the screen only briefly in *Vision Quest*, her performance proved that Madonna's vocal abilities extended far beyond disco.

At top: Just as she is about to recover her missing belongings, Susan is arrested for refusing to pay her cab fare.

Right: Madonna herself supplied the wardrobe for Susan.

Far right: Susan is reunited with Jim, the man who places the personal ads that read 'Desperately Seeking Susan.'

These pages: Scenes from *Desperately Seeking Susan*. The film was a surprise hit, reaping profits much higher than originally anticipated. Fortunately for its makers, the film's release coincided with Madonna's rise to fame.

Madonna Meets the Public

With two hit albums *and* a starring role in a successful film to her credit, Madonna was ready for her first concert tour of 28 cities. The supply of tickets was far less than the demand for them, and when the three shows at 5800-seat Radio City Music Hall sold out in less than a half an hour, larger venues were quickly added to the itinerary.

Opening at Seattle's Paramount Theatre, Madonna danced, paraded and twisted all over the stage in a tightly choreographed extravaganza featuring 13 of her songs. There was nothing demure about her performance as she wrapped her body around the leg of her guitarist. At the end of each concert, attired in a white wedding dress, she returned for a crowd-pleasing encore of 'Like A Virgin,' and asked the audience 'Will you marry me?' Madonna, we love you, was the enthusiastic reply.

Madonna's biggest performance of 1985 was at the Live Aid concert at Philadelphia's JFK Stadium on 13 July. The concert, a fundraiser to fight famine in Ethiopia, was broadcast live by satellite from JFK Stadium and Wembley Stadium in London to more than one billion people around the globe. Wowing the crowd of 90,000 with dynamite versions of 'Holiday,' 'Into the Groove' and 'Love Makes the World Go Round,' Madonna held her own against such legends of rock and roll as Mick Jagger and Keith Richards of the Rolling Stones, Bob Dylan and Tina Turner.

Left: Madonna has always been an attention-getter. Since she first came to the public eye, her penchant for wearing lingerie in ways that most of us have never imagined has never failed to shock and appall, as well as inspire.

Right: Madonna serenades the crowd with one of her many hit songs.

Left: Madonna was one of the featured performers at the Live-Aid concert, the biggest concert event of 1985. This major fund-raising event was held at two locations: JFK Stadium in Philadelphia and Wembley Stadium in London.

Right: Back stage with Rosanna Arquette, her friend and co-star from *Desperately Seeking Susan*.

Little did the audience know that for the first time in her career, Madonna was apprehensive. *Playboy* and *Penthouse* had both featured nude photos of Madonna taken when she had modeled for art classes, and this was the first time she had to face the public since the photos hit the newsstands. Part of her was mortified–control of her life had been taken out of her hands–but in the end she triumphed: 'Part of me felt this big, but another part of me was saying "I'll be dammed if I'm gonna let them make me feel down, I'm gonna get out there and kick ass, get this dark cloud out from over my head."'

Playboy and *Penthouse* hastened to point out that the photos of Madonna were 'artistic.' Nonetheless, she rightfully felt violated. 'At first the *Playboy* photos were very hurtful to me, and I wasn't sure how I felt about them. Now I look back at them and I feel silly that I ever got upset, but I *did* want to keep some things private. It's not really a terrible thing in the end, but you're not ready for it, and it seems so awful and you seem so exposed.'

Madonna was not the first star to be exploited in such a manner. Vanessa Williams had lost her Miss America title when photos from her past came back to haunt her, and Marilyn Monroe was subjected to similar treatment when a calendar featuring nude photos of her was released.

When she took the stage at JFK Stadium, Madonna held her head high. She ignored Bette Midler's none-too-subtle allusion to the photos, gave a terrific performance *and* maintained her sense of humor.

Madonna and Sean

Sean Penn first met Madonna backstage during the taping of the video for 'Material Girl,' and soon they were the most talked-about Hollywood couple since Richard Burton and Elizabeth Taylor. An uninvited guest but a man not easily deterred, Penn was as well known for his belligerent attitude with the press as he was for his films. Nonetheless, he was as curious as the rest of the world about Madonna. A friendship soon developed, but it was hardly love at first sight, and Penn would later tell their wedding guests 'I just remember her saying "Get out! Get out! Get out!"'

Those were words to make a man fall in love. After the initial meeting, Sean picked up a book of quotations, turned to a random page and read: 'She had the inno-cence of a child and the wit of a man.' The words seemed to be an omen, and so the courtship began.

Their stormy courtship offered a glimpse of things to come. Madonna spent a good part of the time on the road with her Virgin Tour, while Sean was in Tennessee filming *At Close Range*. On one occasion when Madonna visited Sean on the set, the couple was approached by two British photographers. In his customary brutish style, Penn allegedly greeted the photographers with rocks. The end result was an assault charge and a $1 million civil suit.

The tabloids scoffed at the possibility that this was true love, citing Madonna's past associations with men who were able to advance her career, but friends of the couple debunked this notion. While it may have seemed they were

These pages: From the moment Madonna met Sean Penn, the press hounded them, following them everywhere they went. Here Madonna and Sean head for a concert at the Roxy in Los Angeles, under the watchful eye of photographers.

Stardom has its price, as Madonna explains, 'You can't affect people in a large, grand way without being scrutinized and put under a microscope, and I accept that.' Sean, however, was less cordial in his relations with the press.

44

Above: Madonna and Sean—they provided more fuel for the gossip columnists than any Hollywood couple since Elizabeth Taylor and Richard Burton.

Left: Unfortunately, jogging together didn't help strengthen their marriage.

Right: Madonna, Sean and friends during one of their marriage's infrequent lighter moods.

opposites–he shuns publicity, she attracts it, he's a serious actor, she's a video vixen with a sense of humor–they were definitely in love, and on 16 August 1985, six months after their first tempestuous meeting, Sean and Madonna were married.

The wedding was held under tight security. Guests were not notified of the location until the day before the ceremony. Reporters could not get past the security checkpoint, and although helicopters invaded their privacy from above, the wedding was a private affair for 220 friends and relatives, ranging from Madonna's seven siblings and her 73-year-old grandmother, to such Hollywood luminaries as Christopher Walken, Carrie Fisher, Diane Keaton and Tom Cruise. Like any other bride, Madonna was dressed in white tulle and lace, her characteristic style of dress subdued for the occasion.

Their marriage, however, would be far from private. The Poison Penns, as they were dubbed by the press, would be constantly in the headlines as Sean battled with paparazzi. One of his brawls led to a $1000 fine and a year's probation, and subsequent incidents would lead to a brief prison sentence for violating probation. Sean's violent outbursts were a source of stress for the singer, and Madonna reportedly sought psychiatric help soon after they were married.

Being the focus of media attention didn't help matters at all. 'A lot of the times the press would make up the most awful things that we had never done, fights we never had,' recalls Madonna. 'Then sometimes we would have a fight, and we'd read about it, and it would be almost spooky, like they'd predicted it or they'd bugged our phones or they were listening in our bedroom.' When Sean wasn't making headlines with his latest fisticuff, there were rumors of pregnancy and divorce. After three years of tumultuous marriage, all rumors were laid to rest when the couple finally did divorce.

Shanghai Surprise

In between his battles with the press, Madonna and Sean traveled to Macao to film *Shanghai Surprise* (1986), a film produced by ex-Beatle George Harrison's Hand Made Films. Set in Shanghai in the 1930s, the film cast Madonna as a missionary who falls for a fast-talking soldier of fortune, played by her husband, Sean Penn. The filmmakers envisioned a romance similar to the one that developed between Humphrey Bogart and Katherine Hepburn in *The African Queen*. Unfortunately, *Shanghai Surprise* did not live up to that standard. Everyone who saw *Shanghai Surprise* was in agreement: The movie was dismal.

The off-camera action attracted more attention than the movie itself, as Sean engaged in his usual tussles with the press. George Harrison flew to Macao to try to make peace between the Penns and assorted journalists, and as a

Left: In *Shanghai Surprise*, Madonna played the part of Gloria, a young woman who has left her home in Massachusetts and the prospect of a safe marriage to do missionary work.

Right: Apparently Madonna's fans were not ready to see the star as a missionary, for *Shanghai Surprise* was a box-office flop.

Above and left: Once in the Orient, Madonna's character, Gloria, meets Mr Wade, played by Sean Penn. A reluctant courtship ensues, but the romance failed to ignite sparks in the audience.

Right: The executive producer of the film was ex-Beatle George Harrison, who was called in from London to solve the disputes between the press and the 'Poison Penns.'

result filming was transferred to London. Knowing the frustration of being constantly in the public eye, Harrison did his best to shield the young couple, prompting Madonna to remark, 'He's great, very understanding and sympathetic. He's given me more advice on how to deal with the press, though, than how to make movies.'

After the movie was completed, however, Harrison's sympathy evaporated with a few harsh words about the pair. 'Penn is a pain the ass,' he was quoted as saying. Of Madonna, he was quoted as saying, 'She has to realize that you can be a fabulous person and be humble as well.'

True Blue

Shanghai Surprise wasn't enough to tarnish Madonna's career. *Desperately Seeking Susan* had shown she was a capable actress, and in the future Madonna would shine both on film and on Broadway. In the meantime, however, Madonna was putting the finishing touches on her next album, *True Blue*.

'Live to Tell' was the first single from the album. Released in May, the song raced to the top of the charts by 7 June 1986. Noted rock critic Dave Marsh listed the song in the top 50 in his book *The Heart of Rock & Soul, 1001 Greatest Singles Ever Made* and wrote 'If there weren't such massive prejudice against Madonna's overconfident displays of sexuality, 'Live to Tell' would be ranked among the greatest pop songs written in the past decade.' The song was featured in the film *At Close Range*, which starred Sean Penn.

In July, the moving 'Papa Don't Preach' was released, and it, too, rocketed to the #1 spot. In the song, a teenage girl pleads for her father's understanding and approval of

Left: True Blue, Madonna's third album, featured the hit single 'Papa Don't Preach.' The video earned Madonna an MTV Music Video Award for Best Female Video in 1987.

Above: Madonna and Sean about the time *True Blue* was released. She dedicated *True Blue* to Sean—'the coolest guy in the universe.'

Right: A publicity portrait made during the True Blue era.

52

Left: Madonna has shown that she can do it all. A movie star, dancer, singer and songwriter, Madonna is also very smart when it comes to managing her career.

Right: The world's most famous dancer in the world's most famous black bra.

her decision to keep her unborn child. 'Papa Don't Preach' illustrates Madonna's maturity as a songwriter. The light-hearted, fluffy lyrics of 'Holiday' are replaced with a poignant portrait of a young girl's agony. The rest of the album harkens back to her disco roots, and as one critic put it, '[the] album remains faithful to her past while shamelessly rising above it.'

By the year's end, the single 'True Blue' was released, peaking at #3. Soon to follow were 'Open Your Heart' and 'La Isla Bonita.' All five of the songs from the album made it to the top five. The album itself sold five million copies and received a Multi-Platinum Award. That's quite an accomplishment, even for a star of Madonna's stature!

These pages: Madonna is known for her videos, which are always innovative and often controversial. Here she continues the theme and the look she created for *Who's That Girl?*

Who's That Girl?

Madonna's third feature film, *Who's That Girl?*, is a modern, screwball comedy made in the spirit of Howard Hawks' *Bringing Up Baby* and Preston Sturges' *The Lady Eve*. As Nikki Finn, a streetwise woman wrongly convicted of murder, Madonna was inspired by the work of Judy Holliday. When Nikki is released from prison, she vows to clear her name, leading to a series of misadventures with co-star Griffin Dunne, who plays the straight-as-an-arrow Loudon Trott. He, of course, falls in love with the wild and wacky Nikki even though he is engaged to be married to his rich boss's daughter. Madonna liked the script from the beginning, in spite of a few flaws, which she believed could be worked out.

Unfortunately, some of the flaws remained in the final product, and the film, like *Shanghai Surprise* before it, flopped at the box office.

Madonna, however, remained enthusiastic about her acting career. 'Acting is fun for me because, well for most people, music is a very personal statement, but I've always liked to have different characters that I project. I feel that I projected a very specific character for *Like A Virgin* and that whole business and created a much different character for my third album.

'The problem is, in the public's mind, you are your image, your musical image, and I think that those characters are only extensions of me. There's a little bit of you in every

Left: Madonna and Griffin Dunne, her co-star in *Who's That Girl?* The pair become embroiled in a series of madcap adventures that are, of course, triggered by the wild and wacky Nikki Finn (Madonna).

Right: Madonna also shared the billing with an unusual co-star—a mountain lion.

58

These pages: The plot of *Who's That Girl?* revolves around the escapades of Nikki Finn. After being wrongly jailed for a crime she didn't commit, Nikki is determined to set the record straight. Her methods, however, have a tendency to get her into trouble.

character that you do. I think I had something in common with Susan in *Desperately Seeking Susan*, and I think I have a lot in common with Nikki Finn in *Who's That Girl?*, but it's not me.'

Madonna's second tour, appropriately named the Who's That Girl Tour, is built around this philosophy. Madonna used seven costumes and a variety of roles and attitudes to compliment the moods of the songs. As the sequence of personas paraded across the stage, the audience

pondered the question and discovered that the answer was more complicated than it seemed.

Dressed in a brazen black bustier, Madonna opened the show as the seductress. As the show progressed, she became alternately comical and thought-provoking. She poked fun at herself by dressing up in a goofy hat and glasses for a few songs, but then turned serious with 'Papa Don't Preach.' Surrounded by images of the pope, the president and the White House, Madonna made it clear

Left: A promotional still for *Who's That Girl?* In spite of Madonna's best efforts, the movie failed at the box office.

Above: Although *Who's That Girl?* bombed, the title song was a hit for Madonna. Originally, the movie was entitled *Slammer*, but the title was changed when Madonna had trouble coming up with a song to fit that title.

Right: A scene from the film.

Left and below: Madonna sizzles on stage during the Who's That Girl tour. As always, the song and dance numbers were guaranteed to ignite the audience.

Right: Madonna has always tried to be thought-provoking and entertaining, and the image of Madonna attired in a brazen bustier while packing a pistol gave the sell-out crowds at her Who's That Girl concerts plenty to think about.

where she stood on the issue of a woman's right to control her own body.

Her performance of 'Live To Tell' didn't use a costume or other props to make a statement, instead drawing its strength from a single, powerful moment at the end of the song, when she slumped to the ground. For a brief moment, the pose suggested despair, and then the singer rose slowly but nonetheless triumphantly.

The Who's That Girl Tour was far more successful than the film of the same name. Approximately two million people on three continents paid top dollar to experience Madonna's musical extravaganza, which reportedly made as much as $500,000 per show. Madonna's challenge to herself was to make a stadium show personal. Anyone who has ever attended a concert at a stadium knows how far removed the audience feels from the performer(s) on stage. By keeping her show visually exciting, Madonna succeeded in making her performance more accessible to the people in the far reaches of the stadium.

An actress, a singer, a song writer and a world-class entertainer, Madonna is also a caring individual who has done benefit performances for a number of causes, from famine to AIDS to rain forests. While on her Who's That Girl Tour, Madonna's Madison Square Garden performance of

64

Left and right: 'I'll make you love me,' she told the audience as she opened the Who's That Girl concert, and she did. The audience never lost interest, never took their eyes off of her. Surrounded by video screens and an elaborately designed set, Madonna alone remained the center of attention in spite of the overwhelming theatrics around her.

Below: A smile on her pretty face, Madonna attends the screening of *Who's That Girl?*

13 July 1987 raised over $400,000 for the American Foundation for AIDS Research (AMFAR). She was the first major star to stage a large-scale fundraiser for this fatal disease, and she would continue to lend her support to fight AIDS with another benefit three years later at the Wiltern Theater in Los Angeles, where she received the AIDS Project Commitment to Life Award.

These pages: Alternately playful and dramatic, Madonna was always prodding the audience to ponder 'Who is that girl?' But the answer always eluded them.

Above: Her voice charged with emotion, Madonna held an enraptured crowd in the palm of her hand.

Right: The glamour girl of the 1980s— Madonna at the 1987 American Music Awards.

70

Madonna on Broadway

In 1988, Madonna shifted gears and appeared on Broadway in David Mamet's *Speed-the-Plow* with Joe Mantegna and Ron Silver, who won a Tony Award for his performance. Mantegna and Silver played two Hollywood sharks hustling a movie deal, while Madonna played an office temp who believed that the book she was reading about how radiation is hastening the end of the world would make a great idea for a movie. She tries to convince the two hustlers that she is right, and although she comes close, in the end, she loses.

In striking contrast to her usual exotic-erotic garb, Madonna takes the stage wearing conservative clothing— a dark skirt, sensible shoes, glasses—and the blonde bombshell was now a brunette. Unlike the brash Susan of *Desperately Seeking Susan* or the crazy Nikki in *Who's That Girl?*, her character was soft-spoken. In other words, she is about as un-Madonnalike as possible.

Though a novice in the theater, Madonna impressed her co-stars and the critics with her self-assurance. 'I like her moxie, she's trying to do good,' said Mantegna. 'She's mesmerizing,' declared director Gregory Mosher.

The audience was equally impressed. At first the audience can't believe it's her, and then they can't believe how good she is. Her performance is flawless, her lines delivered with just the right degree of naivete and earnestness for her character.

Left: Madonna surprised everyone with her decision to appear on Broadway, and the critics were even more surprised when it turned out that this sexy dance club diva proved she could play a serious part.

Right: 'I feel more grounded when I have dark hair, and I feel more ethereal when I have light hair,' says Madonna. 'It's unexplainable. I also feel more Italian when my hair is dark.'

72

Like a Prayer

ike a Prayer (1989), Madonna's fourth album, was her most serious effort in her career up to that point. Her lyrics reflect the difficult times she has had to deal with throughout her life, from the death of her mother ('Promise to Try') through her troubled relationship with her father ('Oh Father') to her failed marriage to Sean Penn ('Till Death Do Us Part'). Though these songs are intensely personal, the themes are universal. 'The emotional context of the album is drawn from when I was growing up—and I'm still growing up.' Balancing these poignant tunes are light-hearted ones like 'Cherish,' 'Keep It Together,' and 'Love Song.' Throughout, the music manages to retain the charm and sparkle that pushed her to the top of the charts.

The title song was the center of controversy. Permeated with sexual and religious symbols, the video enraged various church leaders, who felt it was blasphemous. Segments of the 'Like a Prayer' video were used in a commercial for Pepsi, but the controversy surrounding the video compelled Pepsi to drop the ad campaign. The

Right: The title song from *Like A Prayer* and its controversial video angered church leaders and created an advertising disaster for Pepsi, but Madonna had her revenge. Overseas, the Pepsi commercial was a hit, earning Madonna an international Clio award.

Left: Drawing from the traumas wrought by her divorce and her mother's death when she was a child, *Like A Prayer* was Madonna's most personal album to date.

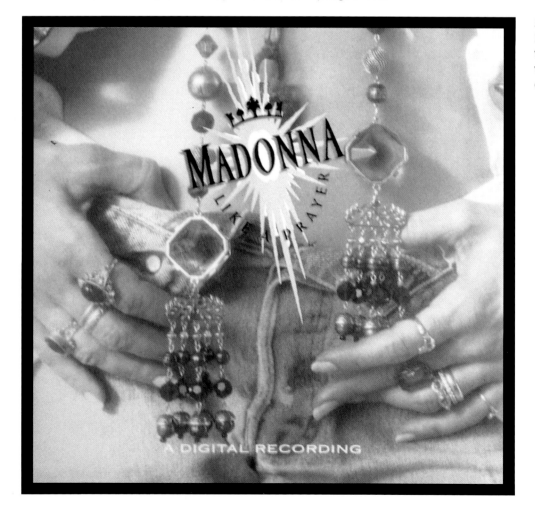

74

change in plans cost Pepsi roughly $10 million. The song itself, however, was suffering no ill effects from the adverse publicity and perhaps even benefitted. 'Like a Prayer' remained the #1 song for well over a month.

'Express Yourself' and 'Cherish' were also released as singles accompanied by videos, with the video for 'Express Yourself' also generating a scandal, albeit on a much smaller scale than 'Like a Prayer.' In this video, Madonna appears briefly wearing nothing but chains and irons. The 'Cherish' video, in which Madonna frolics in the surf, is mild in comparison.

Above: A playful Madonna frolics in the surf for the 'Cherish' video.

Right: Madonna heads for home after a grueling rehearsal. She makes it look easy, but like any professional, Madonna spends hours perfecting her craft.

Dick Tracy

Madonna is a woman of determination, and although her recent acting credits didn't do justice to her skills, she has never wavered in her goal to be taken seriously as an actress. 'I think in the back of my mind, no matter what I was learning to do, I've always had the deepest desire to pursue acting as a career. I guess some would say I'm getting to it in a roundabout way.'

Madonna's acting career got off to a marvelous start with *Desperately Seeking Susan*, but her subsequent roles were unable to match that success. *Shanghai Surprise* attracted more attention with Sean Penn's brawls and *Who's That Girl?* was never able to overcome the flaws in the script. *Bloodhounds of Broadway* (1989), in which Madonna played a saloon singer, was notable only in that it attracted so *little* attention. She was, in the words of one Hollywood mogul, 'a movie star in search of a movie.'

Finally, Madonna found a role that seemed made for her. As Breathless Mahoney in the much-anticipated *Dick Tracy* (1990), Madonna set the silver screen on fire. She was so eager for the part that she worked for union scale–a mere $1650 a week.

With songs by Stephen Sondheim, the part highlighted her singing as well as her acting. By her own admission, however, the part of Breathless was 'not much of a stretch.' For the first time in her acting career she played a villain–a nightclub singer who, in spite of herself, falls in love with Dick Tracy, played by Warren Beatty. The romance is doomed to fail, for they are as different as the sun and the moon, a difference which is illustrated through their costumes, with Dick Tracy in his bright yellow trench coat and Madonna in shimmery silvers and blacks.

The on-screen romance between the two stars continued off screen, giving the gossip columnists plenty to talk about. Like the characters they played, they were an incongruous match, and the romance was short-lived.

Whether *Dick Tracy* lives up to its blockbuster expectations does not really matter for Madonna. Breathless had seduced Hollywood. As Madonna has shown again and again in her brief career, she has that intangible star quality.

She knows, however, that she can't just wait around for something to find her, so has set up a production company called Siren Films to find movies for her. At one point she expressed an interest in acquiring the film rights to the novel *Velocity*, the story of a woman who goes home after the death of her mother to try to develop a relationship with her father.

Left: In *Dick Tracy*, Madonna played Breathless Mahoney, the sexy chanteuse at Big Boy Caprice's (Al Pacino) night club.

Right: Madonna, with her co-star and director, Warren Beatty. For a short time, a romance between the two stars blossomed off screen as well as on.

These pages: As the temptress Breathless Mahoney, Madonna radiated sex appeal, much like the glamorous Hollywood Goddesses of an earlier era.

While sorting things out with her father, the character falls in love with a man who is all wrong for her, and although the romance doesn't work out, she becomes close to her father. The story has strong parallels to Madonna's own life, and in fact, the author, Kristin McCloy, told Madonna that she wrote the story with her in mind.

Rumors have also surfaced that Madonna is being considered for the title role in *Evita* and for a remake of *Some Like It Hot*, with Madonna playing the Marilyn Monroe part and Michael Keaton and Tom Cruise reprising the parts played by Tony Curtis and Jack Lemmon.

It is impossible to predict what Madonna will choose for her next starring role, but one thing is certain. This talented lady is sure to succeed at whatever she does.

Above: As this captivating photo reveals, it's easy to see why Dick Tracy found it impossible to resist the charms of the ravishing Breathless Mahoney. *Right:* Breathless wows the crowd at Big Boy Caprice's night club.

Blond Ambition

While riding high on her success in *Dick Tracy*, Madonna kicked off her third and most imaginative tour to date on 13 April 1990. When tickets went on sale, 2500 were sold in one minute–a new record in the entertainment industry.

The Blond Ambition Tour opened at Chiba, Japan's new Marine Stadium, to enthusiastic reviews. The futuristic outdoor venue at Chiba provided a fitting locale for the show, a highly theatrical extravaganza. The surrealistic atmosphere was heightened by the rain that began to fall just as the show opened. Adhering to the philosophy that 'the show must go on,' Madonna braved the downpour, and although the show had to be briefly interrupted a few times to sweep the rain from the stage, the audience was delighted that the singer was willing to carry on. Three years earlier high winds had forced Madonna to cancel her Tokyo show, and she wanted to avoid another cancellation at all costs.

The tour coincided with the release of Madonna's latest album, *I'm Breathless*, the title of which provides a clever tie-in with her starring role as Breathless Mahoney in *Dick Tracy*. Described on the album sleeve as 'music from and inspired by the film *Dick Tracy*,' *I'm Breathless* is a departure from what Madonna has done before. With the notable exception of 'Vogue,' which seems written specifically for the top 10, the music evokes the era of torch songs and swing tunes. Her voice, too, is different. The bright chirp of 'Holiday' is now deeper and darker. Three songs from the album–'Sooner or Later,' 'Now I'm Following You,' and 'Hanky Panky'–were featured in the glitzy Blond Ambition show.

Madonna's latest tour has been likened to a Broadway production. With the band relegated to the sidelines, the emphasis is indeed on the action that unfolds on the stage. The show brings to life her songs and videos. Her performance is an exercise in precision, a ballet, rather than a

Left: 'With music from and inspired by the film *Dick Tracy*,' *I'm Breathless*, Madonna's latest album, is a departure from her earlier style of music. The cover of the album provided an additional link to the movie by featuring a photo of Breathless and Dick Tracy.

Right: Madonna on stage during the Blond Ambition tour.

84

These pages: As usual, Madonna can be expected to turn heads and even create a furor with her wild style of clothing. The unusual costumes for Madonna's 1990 Blond Ambition tour were designed by French couturier Jean-Paul Gaultier.

rock concert. With its sexy costumes and suggestive banter, it is also is intended to shock. 'Like A Virgin' found Madonna sprawled on a bright red bed. As she rubbed her hands over her body, her two male companions massaged the fake, pointy breasts that were attached to their bare chests. As choreographer Vince Paterson explained, '[Madonna] wanted to make statements about sexuality, cross-sexuality, the church and the like.'

An essential part of the message was delivered by Madonna's exotic costumes, one of which was a pin-striped man's suit with cutouts for her breasts. 'I like the mixing of femininity and masculinity,' explained designer Jean-Paul Gaultier. 'Of course with Madonna, the femininity explodes through the masculinity. It's a little bit surrealistic. It's kind of an obsession in America, you know, the pointed breast.'

Madonna has always been known and even criticized for the blatant sexual imagery of her shows. Her image has invited criticism from feminists who believe that she portrays women in a negative light. Madonna, however, believes that her message is just the opposite. 'People have this idea that if you're sexual and beautiful and provocative, then there's nothing else you could possibly offer. People have *always* had that image about women. And while it might have seemed like I was behaving in a stereotypical way, at the same time, I was also masterminding it. I was in control of everything I was doing, and I think that when people realized that, it confused them. It's not like I was saying "Don't pay attention to the clothes—to the lingerie—I'm wearing." Actually the fact that I was wearing those clothes was meant to drive home a point that you can be sexy and strong at the same time. In a way, it was necessary to wear the clothes.'

In other words, the Boy Toy is not a sex object; she is the boss, the woman warrior, equipped with armored underwear. Blond Ambition is about female power. She does,

Left: Madonna's Blond Ambition tour was hardly a run-of-the-mill rock concert. As her choreographer Vince Paterson explained, 'The biggest thing we tried to do is change the shape of concerts. Instead of just presenting songs, we wanted to combine fashion, Broadway, rock and performance art.'

Right: Even her costumes make a statement. In her rhinestone-studded outfit, Madonna seems to be saying that *dollars*, not diamonds, are a girl's best friend.

after all, knock down her chorus line of men. 'It's a great feeling to be powerful. I've been striving for it all my life. I think that's just the quest of every human being: power.'

The Japanese press concentrated on writing about Madonna's sexual shenanigans to the point of ignoring other aspects of the show, but the response in Japan was a decidedly positive one: Madonna reportedly earned $14 million for just nine shows.

They may have loved her in Japan, but the welcome Madonna received elsewhere was far less cordial. In Toronto, police asked her to tone down her show. When she refused they set themselves up in the stadium with binoculars, presumably ready to rush to the stage and arrest her if she committed any illegal acts in the course of her performance. In Italy, Catholic groups in Rome and Turin called her show vulgar and blasphemous and demanded that Madonna's concerts be banned. Many church officials were especially disturbed by Madonna's routine use of a crucifix as an article of costume jewelry. The reaction was an intensified version of the controversy that had sur-

rounded her 'Like A Prayer' video the year before. Protesters in Italy were successful in forcing the state-run television network to stop running the video.

As is her nature, Madonna held strong to her position. She called a press conference and invited the church leaders to 'Come and see my show and judge it for yourselves. My show is not a conventional rock concert, but a theatrical presentation of my music and, like the theater, it poses questions, provokes thought and it takes you on an emotional journey. This is what I call freedom of expression and thought. By preventing me from doing the show, you would be saying you do not believe in these freedoms.'

Church leaders declined her invitation, but the show went on as scheduled.

Controversy goes hand-in-hand with being an artist. A work of art—be it a novel, a sculpture or a performance—challenges the intellect. As an artist who strives to be thought-provoking *and* entertaining, Madonna has never shied away from controversy, and will undoubtedly continue to do so with her future creative endeavors.

Superstar

Madonna has never been surprised by her success because she worked hard to achieve it. Whether she has been working as a dancer, singer or actress, Madonna has always been determined to succeed. 'I knew I had to apply myself and to work. And that devotion, that ambition and that courage would take me to the next step.'

From the time she was a child, Madonna has always been a hard worker. She helped her stepmother raise her brothers and sisters, all the while maintaining a straight A average. When she first moved to New York, she rehearsed her dancing, learned everything she could about music, and spent hours on the phone trying to make a record deal. She works just as hard to keep herself in excellent physical condition by adhering to a strict exercise program: a six-mile jog in the morning, followed by an aerobic workout and laps in the pool. As she tells her fans, 'Dreams come true'—if you work at it.

Madonna is more than just a talented singer and dancer, and while luck has certainly played a part in her success, she is an extremely shrewd businesswoman. Since 1986, Madonna has made $100 million. In addition to Siren Films, she heads two other companies: Boy Toy handles music publishing, while Slutco makes her videos.

Her greatest talent, however, is that she has mastered the art of being a celebrity. Whatever she says or does attracts attention. She is, quite simply, a star of the highest magnitude, and she will not be forgotten.

Left: Although critics panned *Shanghai Surprise*, Madonna approached the part of Gloria with her characteristic determination.

Right: Superstar Madonna took the world by storm on her Blond Ambition tour.

Left: The superstar on her daily jog.

Above: Bloodhounds of Broadway failed to attract the attention that it deserved. In this scene, Feet Samuels (Randy Quaid) is ready to give everything he's got for the girl of his dreams, showgirl Hortense Hathaway (Madonna).

Right: As fate would have it, *Shanghai Surprise*, Madonna and Sean Penn's lone movie together, was as doomed to fail as their own marriage.

INDEX

Page 96: A young and vibrant Madonna poised on the brink of stardom.

DISCOGRAPHY

Madonna (1983)
Lucky Star
Borderline
Burning Up
I Know It
Holiday
Think of Me
Physical Attraction
Everybody

Like A Virgin (1984)
Material Girl
Angel
Like A Virgin
Over and Over
Love Don't Live Here Anymore
Dress You Up
Shoo-Bee-Doo
Pretender
Stay

True Blue (1986)
Papa Don't Preach
Open Your Heart
White Heat
Live to Tell
Where's the Party
True Blue
La Isla Bonita
Jimmy Jimmy
Love Makes the World Go Round

Like A Prayer (1989)
Like A Prayer
Express Yourself
Love Song
Till Death Do Us Part
Promise To Try
Cherish
Dear Jessie
Oh Father
Keep It Together
Spanish Eyes
Act of Contrition

I'm Breathless (1990)
He's a Man
Sooner or Later
Hanky Panky
I'm Going Bananas
Cry Baby
Something to Remember
Back in Business
More
What Can You Lose
Now I'm Following You (Part I)
Now I'm Following You (Part II)
Vogue

CONCERT TOURS

The Virgin Tour (1985)
Who's That Girl (1987)
Blonde Ambition (1990)

MOVIES

Vision Quest (1985) (bit part)
Desperately Seeking Susan (1985)
Shanghai Surprise (1986)
Who's That Girl? (1987)
Bloodhounds of Broadway (1989)
Dick Tracy (1990)

PLAYS

Speed-the-Plow (1988)